# Bangladesh

by Sweetie Peason

Consultant: Marjorie Faulstich Orellana, PhD
Professor of Urban Schooling
University of California, Los Angeles

**BEARPORT** PUBLISHING

New York, New York

## Credits

Cover, © fotofritz16/iStock and © VikramRaghuvanshi/iStock; TOC, © Hafizur_rahman/Shutterstock; 4, © Munem Wasif/Majority World/AGE Fotostock; 5L, © Munem Wasif/Majority World/AGE Fotostock; 5R, © J A Akash/Majority World/AGE Fotostock; 7, © Dinodia Photos/Alamy; 8–9, © Sjors737/Dreamstime; 9R, © Nazrul Islam/Photo Bangla/AGE Fotostock; 10, © Bridgeman Images; 10T, © Bridgeman Images; 11, © Wikimedia Commons/Public Domain; 12, © Penny Tweedie/Alamy; 13, © palash khan/Alamy; 14–15, © Maciej Dakowicz/Alamy; 15R, © Mark.Pelf/Shutterstock; 16L, © S. Forster/Alamy; 16–17, © RubyRascal/iStock; 18–19, © Muhammad Mostafigur Rahman/Alamy; 18R, © Roop Dey/Alamy; 19T, © Shivang Mehta/Alamy; 19B, © SM Images/Alamy; 20, © Zakir H. Chowdhury/Alamy; 21, © Michal Knitl/Dreamstime; 21T, © ZUMA Press, Inc./Alamy; 22, © RNMitra/iStock; 23, © Design Pics Inc/Alamy; 24, © sta/Shutterstock; 25T, © Matt Mohd/Shutterstock; 25B, © espies/Shutterstock; 26–27, © Farzana Hossen/Majority World/AGE Fotostock; 27R, © Muhammad Mostafigur Rahman/Alamy; 28T, © Tarzan9280/iStock; 28B,© Bayazid Akter/Goto-Foto/Alamy; 29, © CRS Photo/Shutterstock; 30T, © Oleg_Mit/Shutterstock, © Aptyp_koK/Shutterstock, and © Fat Jackey/Shutterstock; 30B, © M Yousuf Tushar/Majority World/AGE Fotostock; 31 (T to B), © Travelview/Shutterstock, © wavebreakmedia/Shutterstock, © Rawpixel.com/Shutterstock, © Photo_DDD/Shutterstock, and © Mallik Photography/iStock; 32, © Sergey Kohl/Shutterstock.

Publisher: Kenn Goin
Senior Editor: Joyce Tavolacci
Creative Director: Spencer Brinker
Design: Debrah Kaiser
Photo Researcher: Thomas Persano

*Library of Congress Cataloging-in-Publication Data*

Names: Peason, Sweetie, author.
Title: Bangladesh / by Sweetie Peason.
Description: New York, New York : Bearport Publishing, 2018. | Series:
    Countries we come from | Includes bibliographical references and index.
Identifiers: LCCN 2017045548 (print) | LCCN 2017046315 (ebook) |
ISBN 9781684025329 (ebook) | ISBN 9781684024742 (library)
Subjects:  LCSH: Bangladesh—Juvenile literature.
Classification: LCC DS393.4 (ebook) | LCC DS393.4 .P43 2018 (print) | DDC
    954.92—dc23
LC record available at https://lccn.loc.gov/2017045548

For more information, write to Bearport Publishing Company, Inc., 45 West 21st Street, Suite 3B, New York, New York 10010. Printed in the United States of America.

10 9 8 7 6 5 4 3 2 1

# Contents

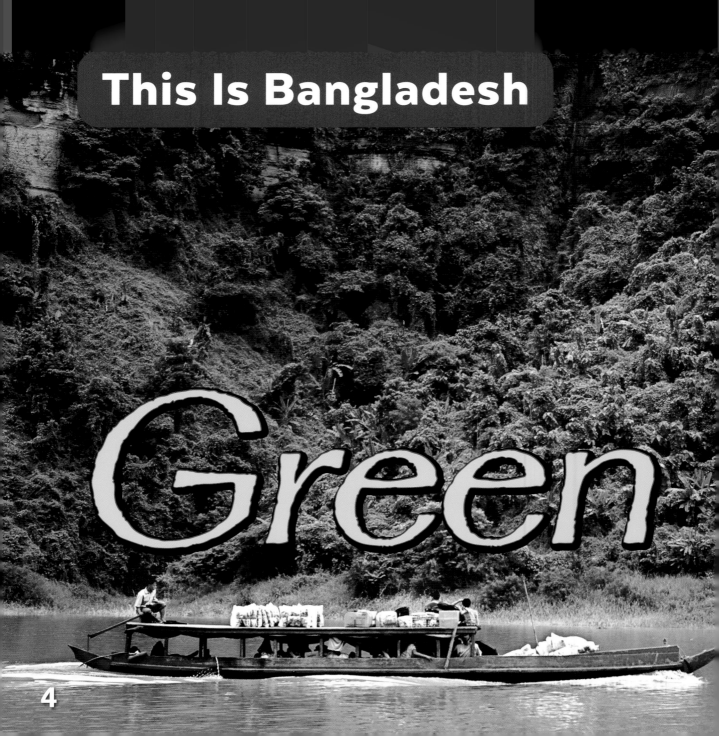

# Green

**Stunning**

FUN

Bangladesh is a country in South Asia.

It's about the size of Iowa.

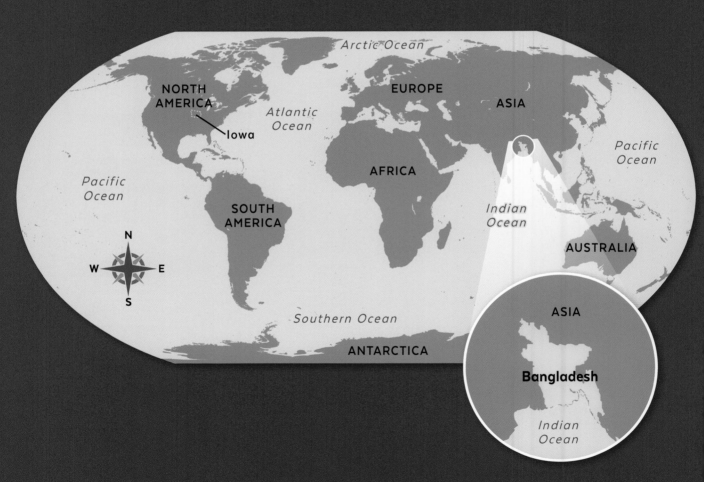

More than 160 million people live in Bangladesh.

Most of Bangladesh is a low-lying **plain**.

Every year, heavy rain falls in summer.

Then Bangladesh's 700 rivers overflow and flood the land.

Farmers grow rice on the flat, moist land.

9

People have lived on this land since ancient times.

a 2,000-year-old statue

stone structures fom Mahasthangarh

Mahasthangarh is an ancient city in Bangladesh. It's more than 2,400 years old!

Over the years, many countries have ruled the area.

These include India, England, and Pakistan.

the city of Dhaka under British rule in 1861

By 1947, Bangladesh was ruled by Pakistan.

Bangladeshis wanted their freedom—and fought for it.

a tank used during the war

During the war against Pakistan, as many as 3 million people died.

Bangladesh became an **independent** country on March 26, 1971!

13

a busy street in Dhaka

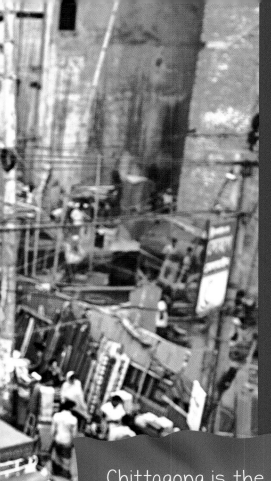

Today, Bangladesh has several large cities.

Dhaka is the **capital** and biggest city.

It has more than 17 million people.

Chittagong is the second-largest city in Bangladesh.

a market in Chittagong

To get around Dhaka, people often ride in rickshaws.

The city is called the rickshaw capital of the world!

rickshaw

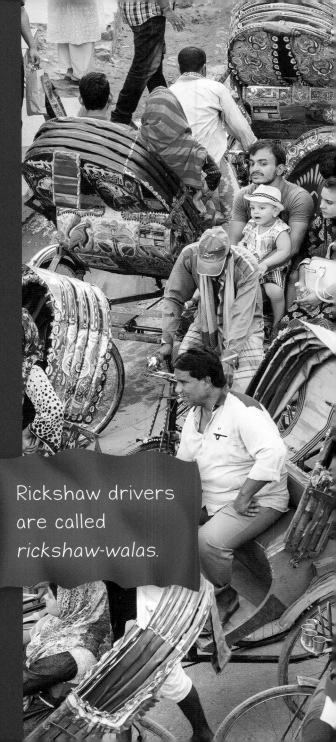

Rickshaw drivers are called *rickshaw-walas.*

The Sundarbans is a vast forest in Bangladesh.

It's also a national park.

Bengal tiger

Bengal tigers and other unusual animals live in the park.

The area includes one of the world's largest **mangrove** forests!

mangrove tree and roots

brown-winged kingfisher

Many religions are practiced in Bangladesh.

However, most people are Muslim.

mosque

They worship at buildings called mosques.

Other people in Bangladesh are Hindu or Buddhist. They worship in temples.

a Buddhist temple

a boy at a Hindu temple

Most people in Bangladesh speak Bengali.

This is how you say *beautiful* in Bengali:

সুন্দর
**Sundara**
(SHOON-dar-uh)

Bengali has its own alphabet and way of writing.

children learning to read and write in Bangladesh

People in Bangladesh eat
a variety of fresh foods.

They enjoy spicy fish or meat
and rice.

Most meals include bread called *chapati*.

A sweet dessert usually follows.

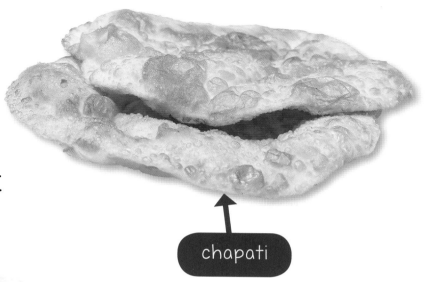

chapati

A famous Bangladeshi dessert is coconut *laddu*. It's made with coconut, sugar, milk, butter, and spices.

Go team, go!

Soccer and **cricket** are the most popular sports in Bangladesh.

Bangladesh's national cricket team is called the Tigers.

Bangladesh has many colorful festivals.

One of the biggest celebrations is Eid al-Fitr.

It marks the end of the Muslim holy month of Ramadan.

people traveling to see family during the holidays

Durga Puja is a Hindu festival. It celebrates the goddess Durga.

29

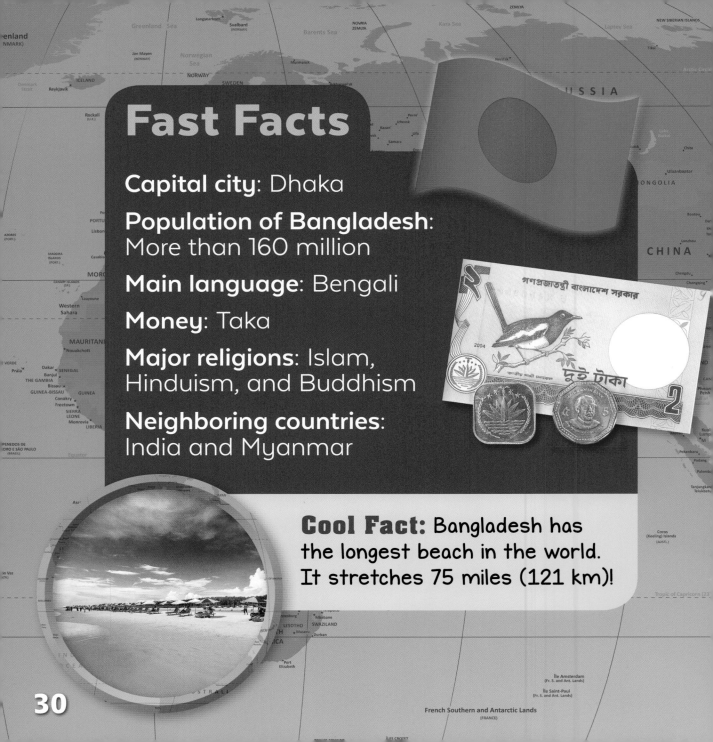

# Fast Facts

**Capital city**: Dhaka

**Population of Bangladesh**: More than 160 million

**Main language**: Bengali

**Money**: Taka

**Major religions**: Islam, Hinduism, and Buddhism

**Neighboring countries**: India and Myanmar

**Cool Fact:** Bangladesh has the longest beach in the world. It stretches 75 miles (121 km)!

**capital** (KAP-uh-tuhl)  the city where a country's government is based

**cricket** (KRIK-it)  a game between two teams played with a ball and bat

**independent** (in-duh-PEN-duhnt) free from the control of others

**mangrove** (MAN-grov)  a kind of tree that grows on land that's flooded part of the year

**plain** (PLAYN)  flat land with few trees

31

# Index

# Read More

**Orr, Tamra B.** *Bangladesh (Enchantment of the World).* New York: Scholastic (2007).

**Rahman, Urmi.** *B is for Bangladesh (World Alphabets).* London: Frances Lincoln (2009).

# Learn More Online

To learn more about Bangladesh, visit
**www.bearportpublishing.com/CountriesWeComeFrom**

# About the Author

Sweetie Peason travels extensively, but she has never been to Bangladesh. Just learning about the food, however, makes her eager to visit.